PINK PAPER SWANS

Written by **Virginia Kroll**   Illustrated by **Nancy L. Clouse**

William B. Eerdmans Publishing Company   •   **Grand Rapids, Michigan**

Copyright © 1994 by Wm. B. Eerdmans Publishing Co.
255 Jefferson Ave. S.E., Grand Rapids, Michigan 49503

Library of Congress Cataloging-in-Publication Data
Pink paper swans / Virginia Kroll; illustrated by Nancy L. Clouse.
p. cm.
Summary: Janetta, intrigued by the paper animals her neighbor Mrs. Tsujimoto
makes, learns the art of origami and becomes Mrs. Tsujimoto's hands when
her arthritis makes it difficult for her to continue.
ISBN 0-8028-5081-2 (cloth)
[1. Origami — Fiction. 2. Japanese Americans — Fiction.
3. Arthritis — Fiction.] I. Clouse, Nancy L., ill. II. Title.
Pz7.K9227Pi 1994
[E] — dc20   93-41093
                                    CIP
                                    AC

Printed in Singapore
Designed by Joy Chu

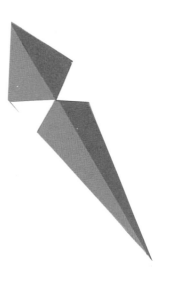

To *Sara DeAnthony*
My origami-doing daughter.
— V.K.

To *Sally, her mother, Kiyo,*
and their Japanese traditions.
— N.L.C.

The city summer steamed and sizzled. "It's an oven up here, Mama. Can I go down to the shadow?"

"Yes, girl, but don't you be botherin' folks or wanderin' off, you hear?" said Mama.

"OK, I promise," said Janetta.

A few folks had already gathered in the shadow that their building cast over their stoop and sidewalk.

Janetta stared at old Mrs. Tsujimoto. She couldn't help it. Mrs. Tsujimoto was doing it again, making things from paper with no glue, no tape, not even any scissors.

Janetta wondered how Mrs. Harris could just keep fanning herself and Mr. Demos could keep on sipping cherry soda. How could Mrs. Santangelo keep her mind on her rosary beads and Bertha and Takia keep playing jacks with this going on right in front of them?

Mrs. Tsujimoto looked up and smiled at Janetta. She bowed forward and handed Janetta a green paper frog.

"Thanks!" Janetta gasped, turning it this way and that. She didn't know what else to say.

She was pleased and embarrassed all at once. She ran upstairs to show Mama, but just before she turned the front door knob, she changed her mind and quickly shoved the frog into her pocket. Mama would be mad, thinking Janetta was bothering folks.

Later, when she was all alone, Janetta took the frog out and
unfolded it, but right away she was sorry she had hidden it
because she couldn't get it back the way it was.

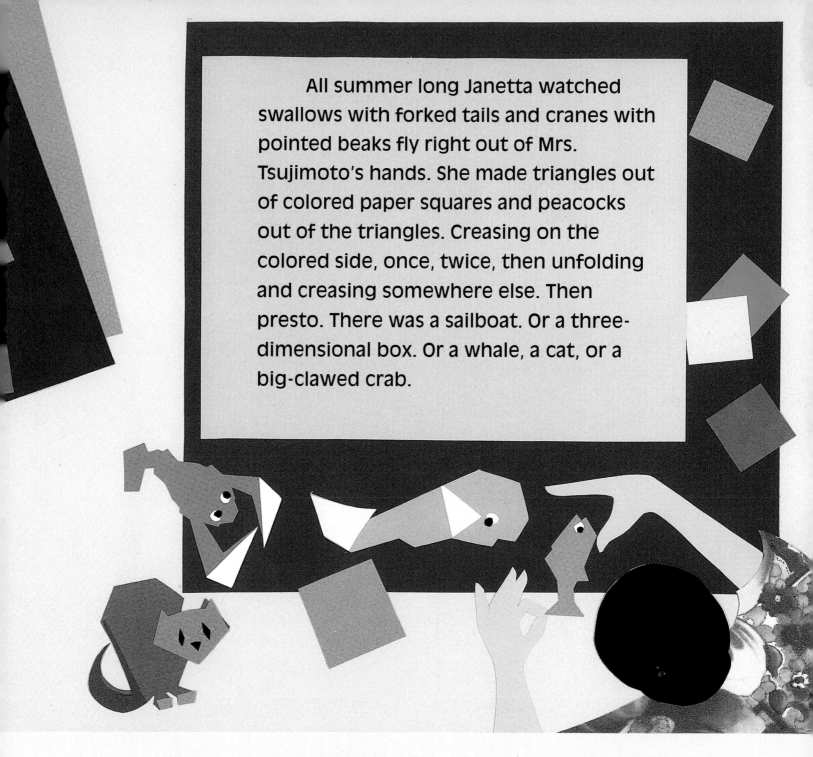

All summer long Janetta watched swallows with forked tails and cranes with pointed beaks fly right out of Mrs. Tsujimoto's hands. She made triangles out of colored paper squares and peacocks out of the triangles. Creasing on the colored side, once, twice, then unfolding and creasing somewhere else. Then presto. There was a sailboat. Or a three-dimensional box. Or a whale, a cat, or a big-clawed crab.

The day before school started, Janetta thought about Mama saying, "Don't you be botherin' folks," but she couldn't help it.

She blurted right out, "My name's Janetta Jackson and I been watchin' you and I'm gonna burst if I don't ask you how you do it, Miz Tsujimoto. That foldin'. I ain't never seen anything like it." She pointed to the orange fish in Mrs. Tsujimoto's lap.

"Ah," Mrs. Tsujimoto sighed, "it is origami."

"Looks like magic, plain and simple, to me," said Janetta.

"Sit down, Janetta." Mrs. Tsujimoto motioned to a vacant chair. Janetta thought her voice was like feathers floating. It matched the softness of her face.

"Origami is an ancient Japanese art," Mrs. Tsujimoto explained. "I have been doing it since I was a very small child. I sell my work at gift shops and at the bookstore on the corner. It is a good little business for me."

She picked up a piece of bright pink paper and began to fold. One corner this way.
Another corner, that.
Folding and unfolding and
folding again
and suddenly. . .
"A pink paper swan!" Janetta cried.

"For you." Mrs. Tsujimoto bowed as she handed it to her.

"Oh, Miz Tsujimoto! Thanks!"

This time, Janetta didn't put the swan in her pocket. And she didn't take it apart.

She took it to school and kept it in her desk. She wrapped it in plastic to keep it clean and set it carefully on top of her English book so that it wouldn't get crushed. Fall turned the world gold, and then winter turned the city steel gray. From time to time Janetta took out her pink paper swan. She looked at it over and over again whenever she needed a summer feeling. She thought of knocking on Mrs. Tsujimoto's door but then thought of Mama saying, "Don't you be botherin' folks."

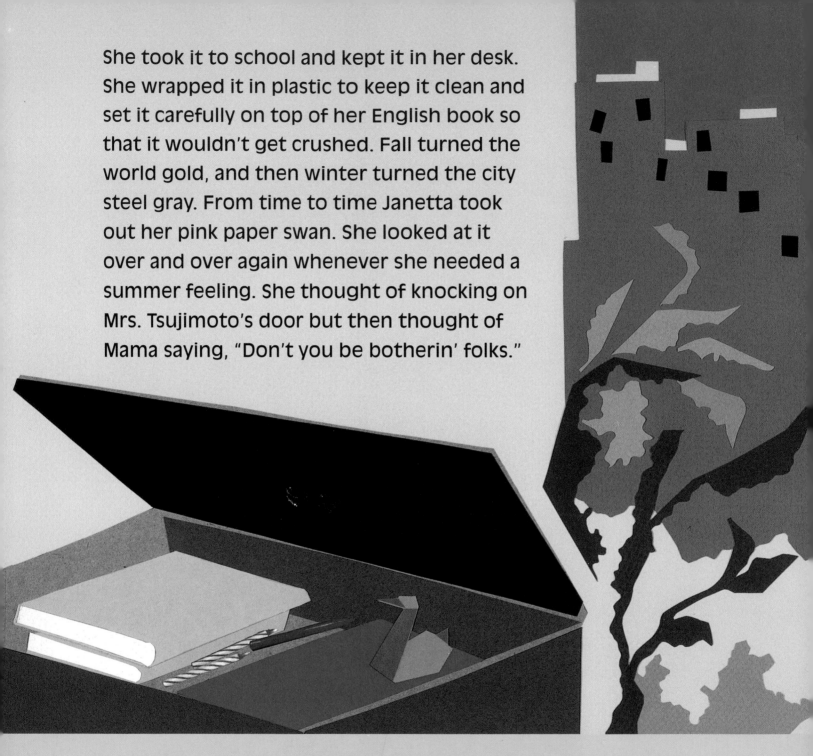

Gradually the geese honked "hello" above the city, buds began to swell on the branches, and it was still light when bedtime came around. The calendar page turned to June, and the schoolbell rang its last until September. Janetta packed her crayons, her smock, her stubby pencils, and what was left of her

eraser into her tattered backpack. She carefully placed her pink paper swan into the safe compartment in front and zippered it closed. When she got home, she put the swan on top of her dresser in her bedroom.

During those first long summer days, Janetta played jacks
and jump rope with Bertha and Takia. She turned sidewalks into
colorful chalkwalks with Jenna and Tyree. She played Wiffleball in
the vacant lot next door with Billy and Yolanda and Raoul because

Mama said that since she was eight she was old enough this year. And all the while, she waited for Mrs. Tsujimoto to come down to the shadow, onto the stoop.

One day Janetta got tired of waiting. She couldn't help it. She found Mrs. Tsujimoto's apartment number on the mailbox downstairs and went up and knocked on door 2D. Soon a feather-soft voice said, "Who is there, please?"

"Janetta Jackson from the shadow," Janetta said.

The door opened slowly. "Come in, Janetta," Mrs. Tsujimoto said.

Janetta looked around. She felt like she had entered a fairy-tale kingdom. Tiny trees of odd shapes in flat pans decorated the windowsills. A paper screen painted with frothy waves and goldfish divided the living room in half. Baskets of seashells sat here and there on the floor. The shiny black coffee table reflected the flowered teapot and matching mugs with no handles that sat on top. A painting of a garden with a waterfall and a tiny bridge hung on the wall.

"I'd love jumpin' into that scene," Janetta said. "Sure would be refreshin'."

"My mother painted it long ago. It was our garden in Japan," Mrs. Tsujimoto told her.

"You lived there? That was your backyard?" Janetta gasped. She couldn't imagine anything but the shadow and the vacant lot.

Mrs. Tsujimoto smiled and nodded. "Sit down, please. I was just getting some tea."

Mrs. Tsujimoto served the tea in the cups with no handles. Janetta felt grown up. It was the first time she had ever had tea. At first they chatted about Janetta and how she liked summer vacation.

Then Janetta wanted to know about Mrs. Tsujimoto and Japan. That's when she found out that Mrs. Tsujimoto was a widow without any children. And finally Janetta asked, "How come you don't come down to the shadow and do that origami foldin' anymore?"

Mrs. Tsujimoto's mouth smiled but her eyes did not. She held up her delicate hands and said, "My fingers do not cooperate any longer. Arthritis is in my joints. Origami gives me pain. Even walking downstairs is painful some of the time, and I do it as seldom as possible."

Janetta looked down. "That's a sad shame." Then she asked Mrs. Tsujimoto about the porcupine fish lamp that hung from the ceiling because she didn't know what else to say.

Right before she left, Janetta said, "Miz Tsujimoto, I still have my pink paper swan. It's on my dresser, right on top."

"I am glad, Janetta," said Mrs. Tsujimoto, bowing slightly. And this time her eyes did smile.

The night grew hot, and Janetta lay in bed, longing for the cool of the shadow. The streetlight shone in the window, making the pink paper swan glow red. A lump came to Janetta's throat, and she thought she might cry. What would happen if Mrs. Tsujimoto couldn't work anymore? What would become of her business?

Suddenly an idea glowed brighter than the streetlight. Janetta's eyes swallowed up the tears again. Her excitement kept her awake as she watched the moon climb into the sky. Finally she fell asleep after too much tossing. She couldn't wait until tomorrow!

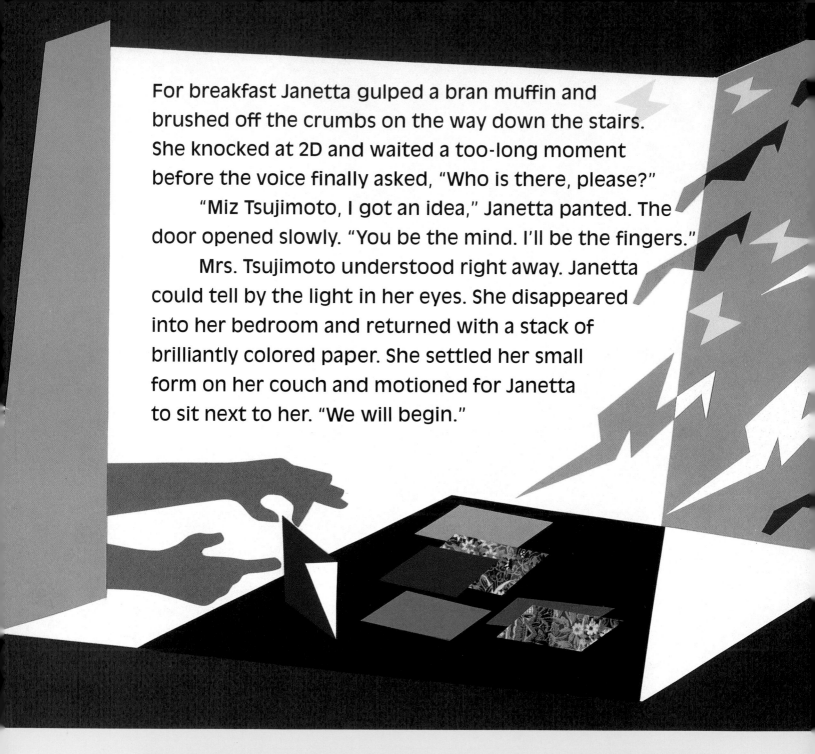

For breakfast Janetta gulped a bran muffin and brushed off the crumbs on the way down the stairs. She knocked at 2D and waited a too-long moment before the voice finally asked, "Who is there, please?"

"Miz Tsujimoto, I got an idea," Janetta panted. The door opened slowly. "You be the mind. I'll be the fingers."

Mrs. Tsujimoto understood right away. Janetta could tell by the light in her eyes. She disappeared into her bedroom and returned with a stack of brilliantly colored paper. She settled her small form on her couch and motioned for Janetta to sit next to her. "We will begin."

Mrs. Tsujimoto nodded, and Janetta took the top piece of paper, the bright red piece. She turned it over to its white side and felt its smoothness. She imagined flocks of red cardinals, yellow butterflies, and snow-white cranes taking off from her fingertips.

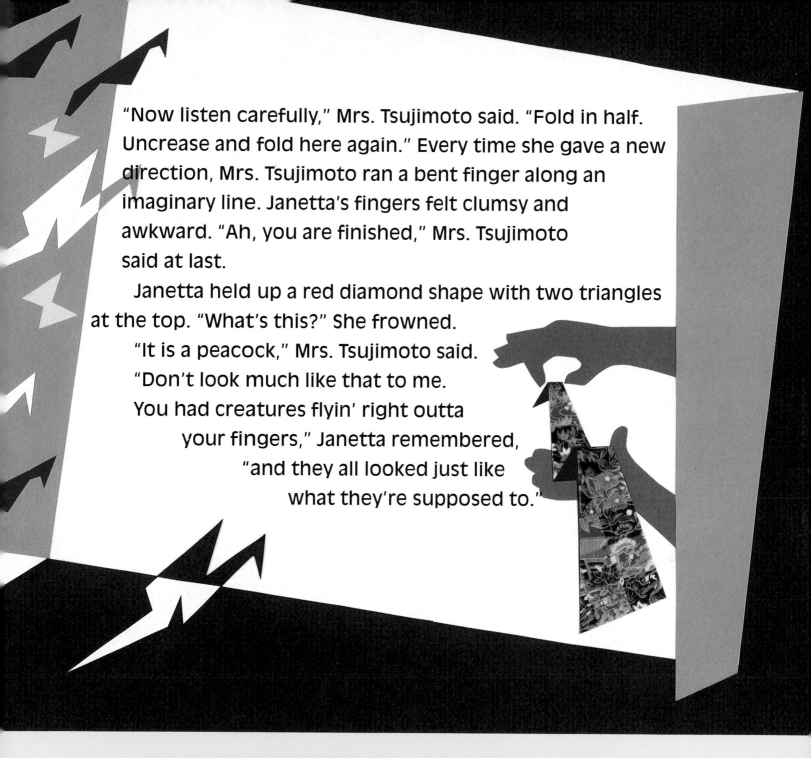

"Now listen carefully," Mrs. Tsujimoto said. "Fold in half. Uncrease and fold here again." Every time she gave a new direction, Mrs. Tsujimoto ran a bent finger along an imaginary line. Janetta's fingers felt clumsy and awkward. "Ah, you are finished," Mrs. Tsujimoto said at last.

Janetta held up a red diamond shape with two triangles at the top. "What's this?" She frowned.

"It is a peacock," Mrs. Tsujimoto said.

"Don't look much like that to me. You had creatures flyin' right outta your fingers," Janetta remembered, "and they all looked just like what they're supposed to."

"Do not be discouraged. Learning origami takes time. You have done very well for the first time."

Janetta cocked her head and looked at her peacock again. "Well, maybe it ain't so bad, if you say so, Miz Tsujimoto."

Janetta worked so hard that morning that she lost track of time and was late getting home for lunch. When she mentioned where she had been, her mother gave her an intent look. "Are you botherin' Miz Tsujimoto?" But after Janetta explained what she was doing, her mother just smiled. "Well, you go on, then," she said.

Each day Janetta's fingers worked alongside Mrs. Tsujimoto's mind. At home Janetta cut paper into squares and practiced alone. Sometimes she felt frustrated. When would her hands know what to do? But one day the folding felt familiar and comfortable. An elegant bird took shape and flew right from her fingers.

Janetta dashed downstairs. "Miz Tsujimoto! Look! I did it!" she cried.

Mrs. Tsujimoto cupped the creation in her crooked hands. "A pink paper swan. It is perfect," she said.

"For you," Janetta said. Mrs. Tsujimoto's eyes filled with tears, but Janetta could tell they were the smiling kind of tears.

"Thank you." Mrs. Tsujimoto bowed. "It will go on my dresser—right on top." Janetta beamed like the summer sun.

For the rest of the summer, Janetta fashioned scores of creatures—flat-finned fishes, pointy-beaked birds, big-mouthed frogs, and, of course, graceful swans.

When there were enough, her mother helped her pack them carefully into bags. Then the two of them set out with the list of shops that Mrs. Tsujimoto had given Janetta. "You need help with these bags," her mother said. "But I think you're old enough to talk to these people yourself."

They stopped at the bookstore first. When Janetta explained to the clerk behind the counter why she was there, the clerk smiled. "You must be Janetta," she said.
Janetta's head snapped up. "How'd you know my name?"

The clerk pointed to a sign in a nearby display case. "Your business partner told us." The sign said

ORIGAMI ORIGINALS
BY
YOKO TSUJIMOTO
AND
JANETTA JACKSON

The same sign was in the display cases in the gift shops, too. On the way home, Janetta's mother had a hard time keeping up with Janetta because she was skipping so fast. The minute they reached their building, Janetta raced up the stairs to 2D to tell Mrs. Tsujimoto her news.

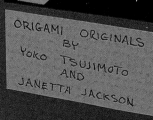

ORIGAMI ORIGINALS
BY
YOKO TSUJIMOTO
AND
JANETTA JACKSON

BOOKSTORE

Mrs. Tsujimoto was standing at the windowsill next to the odd-shaped miniature trees in flat pans. In her hands she held a pair of small pruning shears. She smiled at Janetta. "Have you ever heard of the ancient art of bonsai?"

Janetta laughed and took the shears from Mrs. Tsujimoto's hands. "Ready when you are," she said.

**Here are Mrs. Tsujimoto's instructions.
You may want a parent or friend to help.**

- Use a thin, square sheet of origami paper — that works best.
- Make all creases straight and sharp by pressing firmly.
- This is how to make a *valley fold*: Fold along the dotted line in the direction of the arrow.

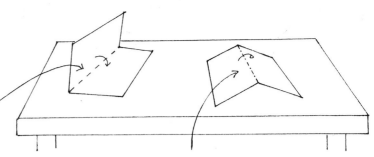

- This is how to make a *mountain fold*: Fold in the reverse direction of the dotted line.

---

1. Place the paper white side up, colored side down.

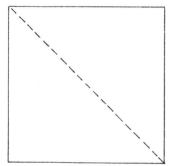

Make a valley fold, then spread the paper flat.

2. Make two more valley folds.

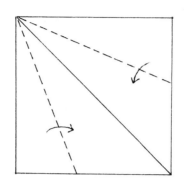

3. Make two mountain folds.

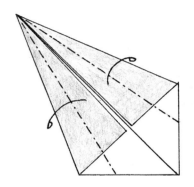

---

4. Make a valley fold down the center crease

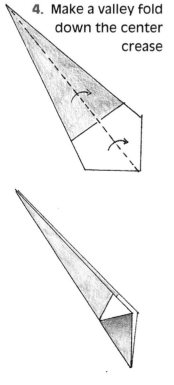

— to look like this.

5. Fold both ways on the same crease

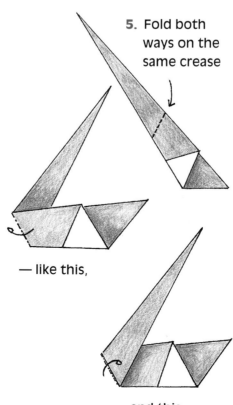

— like this,

and this.

6. Open the center fold.

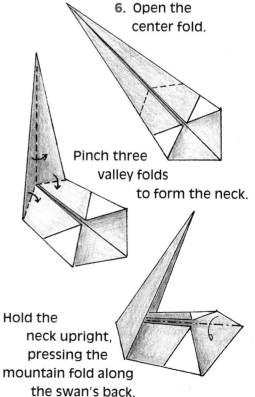

Pinch three valley folds to form the neck.

Hold the neck upright, pressing the mountain fold along the swan's back.

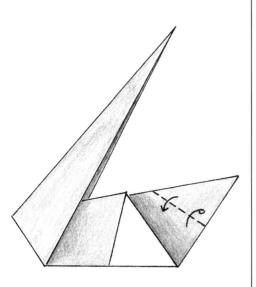

7. Crease the tail both ways
first to the left, then to
the right.

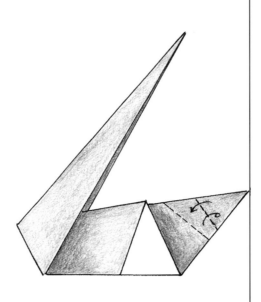

8. Crease the tail again both to the left
and to the right, close to the end.
Notice angle in diagram.

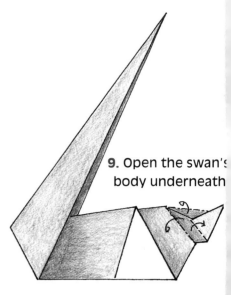

9. Open the swan's
body underneath

Make a mountain fold
on the larger marked crease
and a valley fold on the smaller
crease near the end of the tail.

10. Crease the neck both to the
left and to the right in
three places.

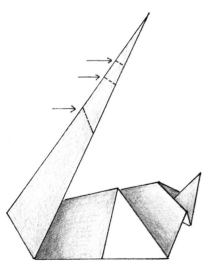

Note angle of creases.

11. Open the swan's neck.
Make a valley fold
by the beak.

Make three
mountain folds.

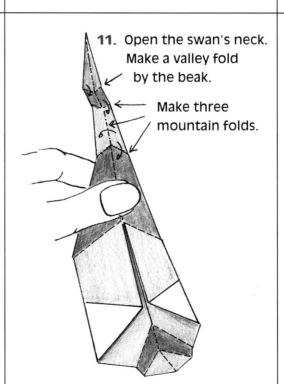

Your pink paper swan is finished.